YOUNTVILLE

# RECIPES
*from the*
# VINEYARDS
*of*
# NORTHERN
# CALIFORNIA

# PICNICS

*Leslie Mansfield*

**CELESTIAL**ARTS
*Berkeley, California*

*When preparing recipes that call for egg yolks or whites, whether or not they are to be cooked, use only the highest-quality, salmonella-free eggs.

CELESTIALARTS
P.O. Box 7123
Berkeley, California 94707

Distributed in Canada by Ten Speed Canada, in the United Kingdom and Europe by Airlift Books, in New Zealand by Southern Publishers Group, in Australia by Simon & Schuster Australia, in South Africa by Real Books, and in Singapore, Malaysia, Hong Kong, and Thailand by Berkeley Books.

Cover and interior design by Greene Design
Cover photograph by Larry Kunkel
Photo styling by Veronica Randall
Public Domain Art thanks to Dover Publications

Library of Congress Card Catalog Number 00-131957

First printing, 2000
Printed in the United States

1 2 3 4 5 6 7 — 04 03 02 01 00

*To my darling nephew*
*GAGE,*
*who is my favorite picnic partner.*

## ACKNOWLEDGMENTS

*Deepest gratitude goes to my husband, Richard, who has helped me with every step—his name belongs on the title page along with mine. To my wonderful parents, Stewart and Marcia Whipple, for their unflagging confidence. To Phil Wood, who makes dreams a reality. To my dear friend and editor Veronica Randall, whose creativity, intelligence, and wit make working with Celestial Arts a joy. To Victoria Randall, for her invaluable assistance. To Brad Greene, for another spectacular design. To Larry Kunkel, for his glorious photography.*

*Finally, this book would not have been possible without the cooperation of all our friends at the wineries who graciously contributed their favorite recipes. I wish to thank them all for their generosity.*

# *Table of Contents*

# Introduction

Just mention California wine country and thoughts of warm sunshine, vines heavy with ripening grapes, and a relaxed lifestyle come to mind. The small villages throughout the wine country each have their own personalities, as do the wineries. From rural, family-run boutique wineries to large, stately wineries surrounded by a sea of vineyards, they all have one thing in common—a love for good food and wine.

This love of food and wine has resulted in an explosion of cutting-edge ideas that have defined California cuisine, incorporating the finest of Europe and Asia while drawing on the incredible local and seasonal bounty.

Entertaining is a way of life in wine country. Whether it is a formal dinner with many courses to showcase a variety of wines, or just drawing off a pitcher of new wine from the barrel to go with an impromptu picnic with neighbors, the desire to share the best they have to offer has helped shape the cuisine of California.

In the following pages you will find recipes offered from the finest wineries of Northern California. Each is a reflection of their personality, whether formal or casual, and all are delicious. Each one is a taste of wine country.

## ATLAS PEAK VINEYARDS

*Atlas Peak Vineyards is situated in an uplifted, hanging valley 1,450 to 1,800 feet above sea level in the Vaca Mountain range that forms the eastern rim of the Napa Valley. Within this subappellation of the Napa Valley, 500 acres of mountain vineyards have been planted to Cabernet Sauvignon, Sangiovese, and Chardonnay.*

*A joint venture between Allied Domecq Wines and Piero Antinori, whose family has a 600-year wine growing history in Italy, Atlas Peak Vineyards has made the production of Sangiovese their specialty and is now the leading producer of this noble variety in the United States. This noble grape, from the Tuscan region of Italy, exhibits delicate aromas and structured tannins and is the wine upon which the cuisine of Tuscany is based.*

# CHARDONNAY STRAWBERRY SHORTCAKE

*Celebrate the first fruits of the summer with Heidi Cusick's delectable shortcake.*

**TOPPING:**

$^1/2$ cup sugar

$^1/3$ cup Atlas Peak Vineyards Chardonnay

$^1/2$ teaspoon orange or lemon extract

$^1/2$ teaspoon vanilla extract

2 pints strawberries, halved

1$^1/2$ cups heavy cream

**CAKE:**

$^1/2$ cup milk

$^1/3$ cup canola oil

$^1/4$ cup Atlas Peak Vineyards Chardonnay

1 teaspoon orange or lemon extract

1 teaspoon vanilla extract

2 eggs, separated

1 cup sugar

2$^1/3$ cups cake flour, sifted

1 tablespoon baking powder

$^1/2$ teaspoon salt

*(recipe continued on next page)*

🦋 Preheat oven to 350 degrees F. Grease and flour two 9-inch cake pans.

**For the topping:** In a large shallow dish, whisk together the sugar, wine, orange or lemon extract, and vanilla extract. Add the strawberries and toss to coat. Cover and chill 1 hour to allow flavors to marry. Stir occasionally.

**For the cake:** In a bowl, combine the milk, canola oil, wine, orange or lemon extract, vanilla extract, and egg yolks and beat until smooth. Set aside.

In a separate bowl, beat the egg whites until soft peaks form. Slowly add $1/2$ cup of the sugar and beat until the egg whites are stiff and glossy.

In a large bowl, stir together the remaining $1/2$ cup of sugar, flour, baking powder, and salt. Pour half of the milk mixture into the flour mixture and beat until smooth. Add the remaining milk mixture and beat until smooth. Carefully fold in the stiffly beaten egg whites, taking care not to deflate them by overmixing.

Divide the batter into the prepared cake pans. Bake for 25 to 30 minutes, or until a tester inserted in the center comes out clean and the top is a light golden brown. Turn out the cakes onto wire racks and cool completely.

Strain the liquid from the strawberries into a bowl. Set aside. In a large bowl, whip the cream until soft peaks form. Slowly add the reserved strawberry liquid into the cream, beating constantly until the cream is whipped.

Place one cake layer on a platter. Top with half of the strawberries. Place the remaining cake layer on top. Top with the remaining strawberries. Spoon the whipped cream over and serve.

*Serves 6 to 8*
*Serve with Atlas Peak Vineyards*
*Chardonnay*

*Wine is music from the vineyard.*
**Marilyn Clark**

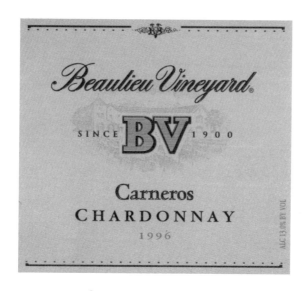

## BEAULIEU VINEYARD

*Beaulieu Vineyard (BV) was founded in 1900 by Georges de Latour, who came from a winegrowing family in Bordeaux. Since its inception, BV has been an important player in the history of California winemaking. Under the guidance of legendary winemaker Andre Techelistcheff, beginning in 1938, BV's famous Georges de Latour Cabernet Sauvignon Private Reserve set the standard for California Cabernet through the rest of the century. Madame de Latour, who ran the company in the 1940s, was a brilliant and outspoken promoter of BV and even had the audacity to show her family's wines in her native France, and won over her countrymen. BV has been a major pioneer of the cool Carneros district of Napa, now legendary for fine Pinot Noir and Chardonnay. The winery is now owned by United Distillers and Vintners North America, and current winemaker Joel Aiken continues the great tradition along with the fine sense of innovation established by Georges de Latour and Andre Techelistcheff.*

# DUCK RILLETTES

*Similar to pâté when served cold, this classic French recipe would be the centerpiece of an elegant weekend picnic. Serve with a loaf of French bread, along with cornichons or another variety of chilled, crisp cucumber.*

1 duck, quartered, with giblets reserved

Salt and freshly ground black pepper to taste

$1/4$ cup cognac

$1^1/2$ cups Beaulieu Vineyard Chardonnay

1 onion, quartered

1 carrot, chopped

1 rib celery, chopped

10 sprigs fresh parsley

2 cloves garlic, chopped

1 bay leaf

$1/2$ cup melted butter

Preheat oven to 425 degrees F.

Place the duck in a heavy roasting pan and season with salt and pepper. Roast for 30 minutes, turning the duck pieces to brown evenly. Remove from oven and transfer the duck to a large pot. Pour the cognac into the hot roasting pan

*(recipe continued on next page)*

and scrape up any browned bits. Whisk in the wine, then pour all pan juices into the pot with the duck. Add the reserved giblets, the onion, carrot, celery, parsley, garlic, and bay leaf. Bring to a boil, cover the pot, then reduce heat to medium-low, and simmer for about 3 hours, or until the duck is very tender and the meat falls away from the bones.

Strain the pan juices into a large bowl. Remove the meat and skin from the bones. Discard the bones and vegetables. Shred the meat into small pieces and finely chop the skin. Stir the meat and skin into the liquid with a wooden spoon. Taste for seasonings, and pepper bring out the flavors. Chill in the refrigerator and stir vigorously about every 30 minutes until the mixture is very stiff. Pack the rillettes into an earthenware crock or terrine. Pour the melted butter on top, cover, and chill for at least 24 hours in the refrigerator before serving.

*Makes about 2 1/2 pounds*
*Serve with Beaulieu Vineyard*
*Chardonnay*

## BELVEDERE VINEYARDS
## AND WINERY

*In Italian, "belvedere" means "beautiful view," which aptly describes the vista from this rustic redwood winery in the Russian River Valley. The winery was built in 1982, the same year owners Bill and Sally Hambrecht bought their first piece of vineyard land high atop Bradford Mountain in the Dry Creek Valley. Over the years they purchased and planted additional estate vineyards in the Dry Creek, Alexander, and Russian River Valleys in northern Sonoma County. As Bill Hambrecht often says, "Our most valuable asset is our vineyards. Good vineyards are as valuable as gold to a winery, and Belvedere has access to some of Sonoma County's best."*

# CORNISH
# GAME HENS
## *with Lemon & Sage*

*These dainty birds are perfect for a romantic picnic for two.*

1 tablespoon olive oil

1 teaspoon minced fresh sage

1 clove garlic, minced

$1/2$ teaspoon salt

$1/4$ teaspoon freshly ground black pepper

2 Cornish game hens

4 fresh sage leaves

1 rib celery, cut into 8 pieces

1 lemon, quartered

$1/2$ cup Belvedere Vineyards and Winery Chardonnay

Preheat oven to 350 degrees F. Lightly oil a baking dish.

In a small bowl, stir together the olive oil, minced sage, garlic, salt, and pepper. Rub the mixture inside and outside the game hens. Carefully loosen the skin on the breasts by inserting a finger between the skin and the meat. Insert two fresh sage leaves under the skin of each hen. Stuff the hens with 4 pieces of celery and 2 lemon quarters each. Truss the legs together with kitchen string. Place in the prepared baking dish and pour the wine over the hens. Roast for about 50 to 60 minutes, or until the juices run clear when pierced with a skewer. Baste often with pan juices. Remove from the oven and let stand 10 minutes before carving, if serving hot.

*Serves 2*
*Serve with Belvedere Vineyards and Winery Chardonnay*

## BENZIGER FAMILY
## WINERY

*The Benziger Family, producers of Benziger Family, Reserve, and Imagery Wines, believes that the nature of great wine lies in the vineyard's character, the winemaker's artistry, and the family's passion. At Benziger this means farming and vinifying select vineyards to mine the unique character of each, winemaking that combines intuition and artistry with a minimalist philosophy, and passion that is shared by the entire family. In its quest for uniqueness through diversity, the family produces more than 300 lots of grapes each year from more than 60 ranches, in over a dozen appellations.*

# HERBED CHICKEN
*Cooked Under a Brick*

*When served cold at your next picnic, the herbs will have time to infuse into this sublime and uniquely cooked main course.*

¹/₂ cup olive oil

¹/₃ cup Benziger Family Winery Fumé Blanc

¹/₄ cup finely chopped fresh basil

1 tablespoon freshly squeezed lemon juice

1 tablespoon minced fresh rosemary

2 cloves garlic, minced

1 teaspoon hot red chile flakes

1 teaspoon salt

¹/₂ teaspoon freshly ground black pepper

1 free-range chicken, about 3 pounds

2 bricks wrapped in aluminum foil

In a shallow dish, whisk together ¹/₄ cup of the olive oil, the wine, basil, lemon juice, rosemary, garlic, red chile flakes, salt, and pepper. Split the chicken down the back lengthwise and splay it open so that it lies flat. Place the chicken in the dish and turn to coat with the marinade. Cover and chill overnight, turning several times.

*(recipe continued on next page)*

Remove the chicken from the marinade and reserve the marinade. Heat a large cast-iron skillet over medium heat. When hot, add the remaining $1/4$ cup of the olive oil. When the oil begins to sizzle, place the chicken, skin side down, in the skillet and place the 2 foil-wrapped bricks on top of the chicken. Cook for 15 minutes, or until the skin is crisp and a deep golden brown. Remove the bricks and turn the chicken over. Replace the bricks and cook for 10 minutes. Pour the reserved marinade into the skillet and reduce the heat to medium-low. Continue to cook for an additional 20 to 30 minutes, or until juices run clear when the chicken is pierced with a skewer. Transfer the chicken to a cutting board and let rest 10 minutes before slicing.

*Serves 4*
*Serve with Benziger Family Winery*
*Fumé Blanc*

## BUENA VISTA WINERY

*Buena Vista Winery, located near the town of Sonoma, was built in 1857 by the storied Hungarian Count Agoston Haraszthy. Known as the "father of California viticulture," Count Haraszthy, after constructing Buena Vista's stone winery and underground cellars, traveled to Europe on a mission to bring back cuttings of European grape vines. These vines, from the greatest vineyards of France, became the source for much of California's early vineyard plantings.*

*Over a century later, in 1979, the Moller-Racke family of Germany purchased the winery and invested in prime vineyard land within the Carneros region. Today, Buena Vista is the largest estate winery in Carneros.*

# LENTIL SALAD
## *with Cucumbers, Tomatoes & Feta*

*Janet Fletcher uses the small gray-green French lentils because they hold their shape when cooked.*

DRESSING:

3 tablespoons red wine vinegar

1 tablespoon Dijon mustard

1 clove garlic, minced

1/4 cup olive oil

1 cup French lentils *(lentilles de Puy)*

8 ounces tomatoes, peeled, seeded, and diced

1/2 English cucumber, peeled, seeded, and cut into 1/4-inch cubes

1/2 cup finely diced red onion

1/4 cup minced fresh dill

1/4 cup minced fresh parsley

Salt and freshly ground black pepper to taste

4 ounces feta cheese, crumbled

**For the dressing:** In a small bowl, whisk together the vinegar, Dijon mustard, and garlic. Slowly whisk in the olive oil. Set aside.

In a saucepan, bring 4 cups of salted water to a boil. Stir in the lentils, reduce heat to medium-low, and simmer gently, uncovered, for about 25 minutes, or until the lentils are just tender. Drain the lentils in a colander. Transfer the lentils to a shallow dish, pour the dressing over, and toss gently. Stir in the tomatoes, cucumber, red onion, dill, parsley, salt, and pepper. Cover and chill for 1 hour in the refrigerator to allow flavors to marry. Remove the lentil salad from refrigerator and stir in the feta cheese. Serve cold or at room temperature.

*Serves 4*
*Serve with Buena Vista Carneros*
*Pinot Noir*

## CANYON ROAD WINERY

*One of Sonoma County's more picturesque settings, Canyon Road Winery is a favorite among wine country visitors. A warm and friendly tasting room features award-winning Canyon Road wines, including some limited selections available only at the winery. Visitors can enjoy a country deli and gift shop, picnic areas by the vines, complimentary wine tasting, and great hospitality.*

# POTATO SALAD

*This traditional American potato salad is the perfect accompaniment to fried chicken for a Fourth of July picnic.*

6 hard-boiled eggs

1 cup mayonnaise

1 tablespoon mustard

2 teaspoons cider vinegar

1/3 cup finely chopped onion

1/4 cup finely chopped dill pickle

2 tablespoons finely chopped sweet pickle

2 1/2 pounds Idaho potatoes, scrubbed

Salt and freshly ground black pepper to taste

Peel the eggs and cut in half. Place the yolks in a large bowl and set aside the whites. Mash the egg yolks with a fork until smooth. Stir in the mayonnaise, mustard, and vinegar and mix until smooth. Chop the egg whites and add to the egg yolks along with the onion, dill pickle, and sweet pickle. Stir until mixed.

*(recipe continued on next page)*

In a large pot of boiling salted water, cook the potatoes in their skins until barely tender when pierced with a skewer. Drain and cool slightly. When just cool enough to handle, peel and cut the potatoes into $1/2$-inch cubes. Add the hot potatoes to the egg mixture and toss to combine, taking care not to break up the potatoes. Season with salt and pepper. Cover and chill at least 8 hours in the refrigerator before serving.

*Serves 6*
*Serve with Canyon Road Winery*
*Sauvignon Blanc*

*Wine ...the intellectual part of the meal.*

**Alexandre Dumas**

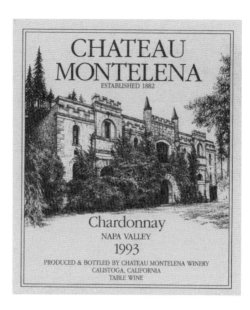

# CHATEAU MONTELENA WINERY

*A visit to Chateau Montelena is a must for wine lovers seeking excellence. With thick natural stone walls, which maintain perfect temperature and humidity for aging wine, and the exceptional grapes that come from their Estate Vineyard, Chateau Montelena has earned its reputation as one of California's first growths. Even the French, for the first time in the history of winemaking, named the Chateau Montelena Chardonnay the world's greatest Chardonnay in 1976.*

# CANNELLINI BEAN SALAD *with* *Olivita Croutons*

*This cold bean salad draws upon the Italian heritage of California's wine country.*

1 can (15 ounces) cannellini beans, drained

6 slices bacon, cooked until crisp and crumbled

1 zucchini, julienned

2 shallots, minced

1 tablespoon minced fresh parsley

1/4 cup white wine vinegar

1/4 cup olive oil

Salt and freshly ground black pepper to taste

OLIVITA CROUTONS:

1/4 cup olivita (recipe on page 85)

3 tablespoons olive oil

2 cups cubed French bread

Preheat oven to 400 degrees F. Lightly oil a baking sheet.

In a bowl, combine the beans, bacon, zucchini, shallots, parsley, vinegar, olive oil, salt, and pepper. Toss to combine. Cover and chill 1 hour to allow the flavors to marry.

**For the croutons:** In a large bowl, whisk together the olivita and olive oil. Add the cubed French bread and toss to coat. Spread out the croutons on the prepared baking sheet. Bake until lightly toasted, about 10 minutes, turning once.

Divide the bean salad into 4 bowls and top with the croutons.

*Serves 4*
*Serve with Chateau Montelena Winery Chardonnay*

# CARDINALE WINERY

*Cardinale Rule: Make grape selection an obsession and gentle winemaking a virtue. Grow fruit of intense vineyard and varietal character from the finest sites in the Mayacamas. Pick only when the fruit is physiologically ripe and balanced in flavor. Hand harvest into small lug boxes, during the cool of the morning. Keep each vineyard separate, in order to know it better. Hand sort all fruit and use only sound, ripe berries. Carefully crack the berries and begin native yeast fermentation. Let juice and skins macerate gently for 25 to 35 days to maximize flavor and texture. Use a traditional basket press to deepen mid-palate flavors. Place into 100% new tight-grained French oak château barrels. Attentively rack wine from barrel to barrel every three months. Age in barrel for 18 to 21 months. Bottle unfiltered. Age in bottle for 12 months before release. Enjoy, or bottle age for an additional 5 to 10 years.*

# ROASTED TOMATO SOUP

*Chefs Tess McDonough and Ed Walsh suggest serving this rich soup with crusty French bread.*

8 tomatoes

1 onion, peeled and quartered

2 cloves garlic, peeled

2 tablespoons olive oil

1 tablespoon balsamic vinegar

Salt and freshly ground black pepper to taste

1/2 cup Cardinale Winery Royale

1/2 cup half-and-half

1/4 cup chopped fresh basil

Preheat oven to 425 degrees F.

In a large ovenproof pot, combine the tomatoes, onion, garlic, olive oil, vinegar, salt, and pepper. Pour the wine over the top. Place in the oven and roast for 45 minutes. Remove from the oven and cool. Purée the mixture in batches until smooth. Pour through a sieve to remove the skin and seeds. Return to the pot, add the half-and-half, and heat through over medium heat. Stir in the basil. Serve warm.

*Serves 6*
*Serve with Cardinale Winery*
*Royale*

## DOMAINE CARNEROS

*Designed after Château de la Marquetterie in Champagne, with its roots in the French house of Taittinger, Domaine Carneros is the only sparkling wine producer using exclusively Carneros grapes for their super-premium méthode-champenoise. Situated atop a knoll surrounded by its vineyards, the château commands a spectacular view of the rolling hills of Carneros. Pinot Noir and Chardonnay, along with a lesser amount of Pinot Meunier, serve as the basis of Domaine Carneros's elegant and delicate sparkling wines.*

# RED, PINK & GOLDEN BABY BEET SALAD
## *with Morbier Cheese Croutons*

*Kevin Simonson takes advantage of colorful tender baby beets when they are in season during the late summer.*

**SHERRY VINAIGRETTE:**

1/2 cup sherry vinegar

1/4 cup olive oil

1 teaspoon minced fresh thyme

Salt and freshly ground black pepper to taste

2 pounds mixed baby beets, red, pink, and golden, scrubbed

Juice of 1 lemon

1 tablespoon olive oil

Salt and freshly ground black pepper to taste

1 fennel bulb, thinly sliced

4 ounces Morbier cheese, thinly sliced

12 thin slices sourdough baguette

8 ounces mixed baby greens

1/3 cup lightly toasted walnuts, coarsely chopped

*(recipe continued on next page)*

🍂 **For the vinaigrette:** In a bowl, whisk together the vinegar, olive oil, thyme, salt, and pepper. Set aside.

In a large pot, cook the beets in salted water over medium heat until tender. Drain and cool slightly. When cool enough to handle, peel and slice the beets into $1/4$-inch slices. Toss the warm beets with the vinaigrette. Set aside to cool completely. In a small bowl, whisk together the lemon juice, 1 tablespoon olive oil, salt, and pepper. Add the sliced fennel and toss to coat. Set aside.

Preheat oven to 425 degrees F. Arrange the cheese slices on the baguette slices. Place the baguette slices on a baking sheet and bake for about 10 minutes or until the baguettes are golden brown and the cheese is bubbly.

Divide the greens onto 6 plates. Top with the beets and drizzle with the vinaigrette. Spoon the fennel on top of the beets. Top with 2 cheese croutons and sprinkle with walnuts.

*Serves 6*
*Serve with Domaine Carneros*
*Le Rêve Sparkling Wine*

## DRY CREEK
## VINEYARD

*Dry Creek Vineyard was the first new winery to be established in the Dry Creek Valley of Sonoma after Prohibition. Synonymous with fine winemaking, Dry Creek Vineyard draws upon over 35 different vineyards to produce their wines, matching the particular soils and microclimates of each site to the varieties that do best in the Dry Creek Valley.*

# LAMB-STUFFED ONIONS

*I imagine a Greek festival was the inspiration for these robust and hearty stuffed onions from Bradley Wallace.*

6 large onions, peeled

2 tablespoons olive oil

1¹/2 teaspoons cinnamon

¹/2 teaspoon thyme

1 pound ground lamb

Zest of 1 lemon, finely minced

¹/2 cup fresh bread crumbs

¹/2 cup ricotta cheese

Salt and freshly ground black pepper to taste

1 tablespoon butter

1 tablespoon all-purpose flour

1 cup chicken stock

¹/4 cup Dry Creek Vineyard Merlot

3 tablespoons tomato paste

Preheat oven to 350 degrees F. Lightly oil a 2¹/2-quart covered baking dish.

Bring a large pot of salted water to a boil. Add the whole onions and cook for 15 minutes. Drain and cool. Remove a slice from the tops of each onion and scoop out the center, leaving a $1/2$-inch shell. Place the onion shells in the prepared baking dish. Set aside.

Finely chop $1/2$ cup of the onion centers. In a large skillet, heat the olive oil over medium heat. Add the chopped onion, cinnamon, and thyme and sauté until the onion is lightly browned. Add the lamb and lemon zest and sauté until the lamb is cooked through. Remove from the heat, stir in the bread crumbs and ricotta cheese, and season with salt and pepper. Stuff the onion shells with the lamb mixture.

In a saucepan, melt the butter over medium heat. Whisk in the flour and cook until bubbly. Whisk in the chicken stock, wine, and tomato paste and simmer, whisking constantly, until slightly thickened. Pour over the stuffed onions.

Cover the baking dish and bake for about 40 minutes, or until very tender. Baste occasionally. Serve hot or at room temperature.

*Serves 6*
*Serve with Dry Creek Vineyard*
*Merlot*

# FERRARI-CARANO
# VINEYARDS AND WINERY

*Villa Fiore, or "House of Flowers," at Ferrari-Carano is one of the most spectacular wineries and visitors' centers in the northern California wine country. Designed to reflect the proud Italian heritage of the Carano family, Villa Fiore houses state-of-the-art kitchens, which are used to educate professionals as well as consumers in the enjoyment of Ferrari-Carano wines. Ferrari-Carano draws its grapes from fourteen winery-owned vineyards over a 50-mile area, from Alexander Valley in the north to the Carneros district in the south. This exceptional supply of fruit allows the winemaker to produce the highly stylized wines for which Ferrari-Carano is known.*

# ONION FRITTATA

*Sit under an olive tree, enjoy a glass of chilled
Fumé Blanc, and savor this delectable frittata.*

8 eggs

3 tablespoons freshly grated Parmesan cheese

2 tablespoons freshly grated Asiago cheese

1/4 cup olive oil

1/3 cup chopped pancetta

2 onions, thinly sliced

1/3 cup chopped prosciutto

2 teaspoons minced fresh mint

4 tomatoes, peeled, seeded, and diced

Salt and freshly ground black pepper to taste

In a large bowl, whisk together the eggs,
Parmesan, and Asiago. Set aside.

In a large nonstick skillet, heat 1 tablespoon of
the olive oil over medium heat. Add the pancetta
and sauté until crisp. Add the onions, prosciutto,
and mint and sauté until the onions are tender. Add
the tomatoes and sauté until tender. Add the onion
mixture to the egg mixture and stir until just combined. Season with salt and pepper.

Preheat broiler.

*(recipe continued on next page)*

In a large nonstick skillet, heat the remaining olive oil over high heat. When the oil begins to sizzle pour in the egg-onion mixture. Reduce heat to low and cook until the underside of the frittata is crisp and golden and the eggs are set. Place the frittata under the broiler to brown the top. Carefully slide the frittata onto a plate and let cool before slicing into wedges.

*Serves 6*
*Serve with Ferrari-Carano Winery*
*Fumé Blanc*

*Therefore God give thee of the dew*
*of heaven, and the fatness of the earth,*
*and plenty of corn and wine.*

**Genesis**

**CHARDONNAY**
SONOMA COUNTY

ALC. 13.5% BY VOL.

## GEYSER PEAK WINERY

*Located just north of Healdsburg, 100-year-old Geyser Peak Winery's tradition of excellence shows in their being named "1998 Winery of the Year" by* Wine & Spirits *magazine and the San Francisco International Wine Competition. Their original vine-covered stone winery is now the cornerstone of a state-of-the-art complex that is one of the most well equipped wineries in California. Within the winery, president and head winemaker Daryl Groom oversees the vinification of not only their sought-after reserve wines but also a multitude of great wines for all occasions.*

# POZOLE

*Ladle into an insulated container and enjoy this heartwarming pozole on a chilly autumn day.*

1/3 cup olive oil

1 onion, chopped

4 cloves garlic, minced

1/4 teaspoon hot red chile flakes

1 cup all-purpose flour

Salt and freshly ground black pepper
      to taste

1 pound lean pork, cut into 1/4-inch cubes

1 cup Geyser Peak Winery Chardonnay

6 cups chicken stock

1 can (29-ounces) white hominy, drained
      and rinsed

2 tomatoes, diced

1/4 cup chopped cilantro

Juice of 1 lime

1 1/2 teaspoons dried oregano

Chopped onion

Chopped cilantro

Lime wedges

In a large pot, heat 2 tablespoons of the olive oil over medium heat. Add the onion and sauté until just tender. Add the garlic and red chile flakes and sauté until fragrant. Transfer to a bowl and set aside.

In a shallow dish, stir together the flour, salt, and pepper. Dredge the pork cubes in the flour mixture and shake off the excess. Add the remaining olive oil to the pot, add the pork, and brown on all sides. Return the onion mixture to pot. Stir in the wine, whisking up any browned bits. Stir in the chicken stock, hominy, tomatoes, 1/4 cup cilantro, lime juice, and oregano, and adjust the salt and pepper to taste. Bring to a boil, then reduce heat to medium-low. Cover and simmer about 1 hour, or until pork and hominy are very tender. Ladle into bowls and serve with chopped onion, cilantro, and lime wedges.

*Serves 6*
*Serve with Geyser Peak Winery*
*Chardonnay*

## FETZER VINEYARDS

*"Live right, Eat right, Pick the right grapes,"* [TM] *signifies the Fetzer Vineyards philosophy toward wine production and living in general. Fetzer has dedicated itself to being an environmentally and socially conscious grower, producer, and marketer of wines of the highest quality, and, to that end, farms 360 acres of certified organic grapes. Their award-winning wines run the gamut from Johannisberg Riesling to Reserve Cabernet Sauvignon. Based in Mendocino County, Fetzer is one of the north coast's finest producers of premium wine.*

# QUAIL SALAD
## *with Yogurt & Grapefruit Vinaigrette*

*John Ash is one of the culinary icons of the wine country. His quail salad is perfect at a picnic on a hot summer day.*

### MARINADE:

2 tablespoons olive oil

1 cup finely chopped onion

$^1/_4$ cup sherry vinegar

$^1/_4$ cup finely chopped fresh mint

2 teaspoons whole white peppercorns

$^1/_2$ teaspoon salt

$^1/_4$ teaspoon freshly ground black pepper

$^1/_4$ teaspoon ground cloves

8 boned quail

*(recipe continued on next page)*

## YOGURT AND GRAPEFRUIT VINAIGRETTE:

1 1/4 cups plain yogurt

1/4 cup ruby grapefruit juice

1/4 cup chopped fresh mint

1/4 cup sherry vinegar

2 tablespoons olive oil

2 tablespoons walnut oil

1 1/2 tablespoons honey

1 tablespoon minced shallot

Salt and freshly ground white pepper to taste

4 cups arugula

1 grapefruit, peeled and sectioned

1 orange, peeled and sectioned

1 tangerine, peeled and sectioned

 **For the marinade:** In a skillet or sauté pan, heat the olive oil over medium heat. Add the onion and sauté until translucent. Whisk in the sherry vinegar, then remove from the heat and cool. Stir in the mint, white peppercorns, salt, black pepper, and cloves. Pour into a shallow dish. Add the quail and turn to coat. Cover and chill overnight, turning occasionally.

**For the vinaigrette:** In a bowl, combine the yogurt, grapefruit juice, mint, sherry vinegar, olive oil, walnut oil, honey, shallot, salt, and white pepper. Whisk until smooth. Cover and chill at least 2 hours in the refrigerator to allow flavors to marry.

Prepare a medium-hot charcoal fire in the grill. Remove the quail from the marinade and grill until cooked through.

Divide the arugula onto 4 plates. Place the grilled quail on the arugula and spoon the vinaigrette over. Garnish with grapefruit sections, orange sections, and tangerine sections.

*Serves 4*
*Serve with Fetzer Vineyards*
*Fumé Blanc*

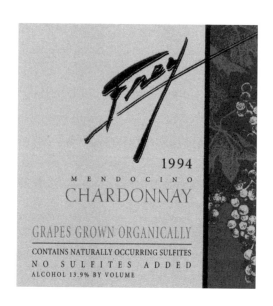

1994

MENDOCINO

CHARDONNAY

GRAPES GROWN ORGANICALLY

CONTAINS NATURALLY OCCURRING SULFITES
NO SULFITES ADDED
ALCOHOL 13.9% BY VOLUME

## FREY VINEYARDS

A *member of California Certified Organic Farmers, Frey Vineyards was one of the first to farm their vineyards organically and offer a wine from certified organically grown grapes. Located near the northern-most origins of the Russian River water-shed, this Mendocino-appellation winery produces elegant, well-structured wines from its dry-farmed vineyards.*

# CILANTRO-PESTO SPREAD

*Tamara Frey serves this delicious spread with hearty whole-grain bread.*

1 bunch cilantro, leaves only

2 tablespoons freshly grated Parmesan cheese

2 tablespoons toasted pine nuts

2 cloves garlic, chopped

2 teaspoons freshly squeezed lime juice

8 ounces cream cheese

2 tablespoons olive oil

In the bowl of a food processor, combine the cilantro, Parmesan cheese, pine nuts, garlic, and lime juice. Pulse until the cilantro is finely chopped, scraping the sides frequently. Add the cream cheese and process until smooth. With the motor running, add the olive oil in a thin stream until it is all incorporated. Cover and chill for 1 hour in the refrigerator to allow the flavors to marry.

> *Serves 6*
> *Serve with Frey Vineyards*
> *Chardonnay*

## GLEN ELLEN WINERY

*Glen Ellen Winery was created in 1983 by the Benziger family with the idea of producing inexpensive and delicious varietal wines to an increasing number of wine consumers. Thus was born the whole category of "fighting varietals." The winery is located in Sonoma, California, with a wonderful visitors' center situated in the charming town of Glen Ellen in the historic Valley of the Moon. In 1994, the Benzigers sold the winery to United Distillers and Vintners. UDV continues to produce Glen Ellen Proprietors Reserve wines with the same degree of dedication to quality—not surprising, as the winemaking team has virtually remained the same for nearly a decade. Glen Ellen utilizes an innovative program, the Grower Feedback Loop, to encourage their many growers to improve the quality of the fruit produced each year to meet the growing sophistication of consumers.*

# ANTIPASTO PASTA SALAD

*This is a great keeper, so don't be afraid to make an extra-large batch of this pasta salad.*

## DRESSING:

3/4 cup balsamic vinegar

3 cloves garlic, minced

2 teaspoons basil, crushed in a mortar and pestle

2 teaspoons oregano, crushed in a mortar and pestle

1 teaspoon rosemary, crushed in a mortar and pestle

1 teaspoon salt

1/2 teaspoon freshly ground black pepper

1/2 teaspoon hot red chile flakes

3/4 cup olive oil

1 pound spiral pasta, cooked in boiling salted water until al dente, then drained

1 1/2 cups Kalamata olives, pitted and diced

1 1/2 cups diced salami

1 cup marinated artichoke hearts, drained and diced

1 cup peperoncinis, seeded and diced

1 1/2 cups diced mozzarella

*(recipe continued on next page)*

 **For the dressing:** In a large bowl, whisk together the balsamic vinegar, garlic, basil, oregano, rosemary, salt, pepper, and red chile flakes. Slowly whisk in the olive oil. Let stand for 30 minutes to allow the flavors to marry.

Add the hot pasta to the dressing and toss to coat well. Add the Kalamata olives, salami, artichoke hearts, and peperoncinis and toss to combine. Let the pasta salad cool completely, tossing occasionally. Stir in the mozzarella. Cover and chill overnight.

*Serves 6 to 8*
*Serve with Glen Ellen Winery*
*Sauvignon Blanc*

## GLORIA FERRER
## CHAMPAGNE CAVES

*Founded by José Ferrer, son of Pedro Ferrer Bosch, the Spanish-Catalan founder of Freixenet, Gloria Ferrer Champagne Caves was opened to the public in July of 1986. Named for José Ferrer's beloved wife, Gloria, the winery has been winning awards and the accolades of wine critics ever since. Located within the cool Carneros appellation, the beautiful building with stucco walls, arched windows, and overhanging balconies is a piece of the proud history of old Spain.*

# COCONUT CHOCOLATE CHIP COOKIES

*These cookies are an excellent way to finish off a great picnic.*

1 cup butter, softened

1 cup brown sugar

$1/2$ cup granulated sugar

2 eggs

1 teaspoon vanilla extract

2 cups all-purpose flour

1 teaspoon baking powder

1 teaspoon baking soda

1 teaspoon salt

1 cup chocolate chips

1 cup sweetened grated coconut

Preheat oven to 375 degrees F.

In a large bowl, cream together the butter, brown sugar, and white sugar until light and fluffy. Beat in the eggs, add the vanilla and beat until smooth. Beat in the flour, baking powder, baking soda, and salt and beat until smooth. Stir in the chocolate chips and coconut.

Drop 2 tablespoons of dough 2 inches apart on a baking sheet. Bake for about 10 minutes, then cool on the baking sheet for 5 minutes before transferring to a rack.

*Makes 24 cookies*
*Serve with Gloria Ferrer Champagne Caves*
*Blanc de Noirs*

## HANDLEY CELLARS

*Known as much for her exquisite sparkling wines as for superbly crafted still wines, Milla Handley practices her craft at the cellars she and her husband, Rex McClellan, founded in 1975. Set in the northwest end of the Anderson Valley, protected to the west by red-wood-covered coastal ridges and to the east by oak-studded hills, Handley Cellars is situated in a unique viticultural region. The Mendocino appellation, by virtue of its cool foggy nights and gentle summers, is ideally suited to the production of aromatic and delicate whites, luscious and elegant reds, and crisp and flavorful sparklers.*

# GRILLED SHRIMP, AVOCADO & CORN SALSA

*Grilling the shrimp adds a wonderful smoky flavor to the salsa.*

6 ounces large raw shrimp

1 tablespoon olive oil

Salt and freshly ground black pepper to taste

6 Roma tomatoes, seeded and chopped

1/2 cup corn kernels

1 red bell pepper, chopped

4 scallions, chopped

1 jalapeño chile, seeded and minced

1/4 cup freshly squeezed lime juice

1/2 teaspoon salt

1/4 teaspoon cayenne

2 avocados, diced

*(recipe continued on next page)*

Prepare a hot fire in the grill. Brush the shrimp with the olive oil and season with salt and pepper. Grill the shrimp on both sides until cooked through. Let cool, then coarsely chop.

In a large bowl, combine the chopped shrimp, tomatoes, corn, bell pepper, scallions, jalapeno, lime juice, 1/2 teaspoon salt, and cayenne and toss to combine. Cover and chill for 30 minutes in the refrigerator to allow flavors to marry.

Stir in the diced avocado and serve with tortilla chips.

*Serves 6*
*Serve with Handley Cellars*
*Gewürztraminer*

# KENDALL-JACKSON WINERY

*In 1974, Jess Jackson and his family purchased an 85-acre pear ranch near Lakeport in Northern California. By 1982, the ranch was a vineyard, the barn was a tasting room, and the pasture was a winery. Meanwhile, they studied the premium vineyards that span California's cool coastal growing regions and discovered the wonderful spectrum of flavors produced by the same grape varietal grown in different locations. Why not use this exciting diversity? Why not blend the best grapes from the best vineyards to produce unique wines with layers of depth and complexity? Their first Chardonnay was made in 1982, from vineyards in Santa Barbara, Monterey, Sonoma, and Lake Counties. This wine was named "Best American Chardonnay" by the American Wine Competition. Their concept of blending the best with the best was affirmed and to this day continues to be the reason their wines are noted for their consistency and complexity, vintage after vintage.*

# SMOKED CHICKEN
## *& Tropical Fruit Salad*

*Tess McDonough and Ed Walsh created this refreshing salad to show off the superb Kendall-Jackson Chardonnay.*

4 cups diced smoked chicken

1 cup diced mango

1 cup diced papaya

$1/2$ cup finely diced red onion

$1/2$ cup finely diced jicama

2 tablespoons freshly squeezed lemon juice

2 tablespoons freshly squeezed lime juice

2 tablespoons chopped fresh parsley

1 tablespoon chopped cilantro

Salt and freshly ground black pepper to taste

1 baguette, thinly sliced

In a large bowl, combine the chicken, mango, papaya, red onion, and jicama and toss to combine. In a small bowl, stir together the lemon juice, lime juice, parsley, cilantro, salt, and pepper. Pour over the salad and toss gently to mix. Cover and chill for 1 hour in the refrigerator to allow the flavors to marry. Serve with the thinly sliced baguette.

*Serves 6*
*Serve with Kendall-Jackson Winery*
*Chardonnay*

*I cook with wine, sometimes*
*I even add it to the food!*
**Leslie Duncan**

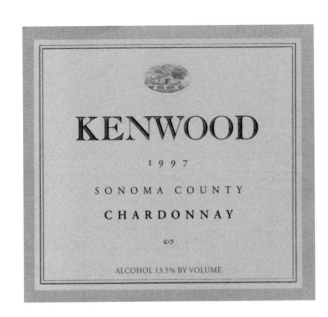

## KENWOOD VINEYARDS
## AND WINERY

*At Kenwood Vineyards and Winery each vineyard lot is handled separately within the winery to preserve its individuality. Such "small lot" winemaking allows the winemaker to bring each lot of wine to its fullest potential. This style of winemaking is evident in the quality of Kenwood's special bottlings. From the Jack London Vineyard series, whose grapes come from the historical lava-terraced vineyards of the Jack London Ranch, to the Artist Series Cabernet Sauvignon, whose labels each year feature the work of a renowned artist, Kenwood shows Sonoma County at its best.*

# SHIITAKE MUSHROOM & GOAT CHEESE PHYLLO TRIANGLES

*These treats from Kenwood's Linda Kittler are excellent both warm from the oven or cold out of the picnic hamper.*

¹/₄ cup butter

¹/₂ cup minced shallots

1 pound fresh shiitake mushrooms, minced

1¹/₂ cups chicken stock

2 teaspoons thyme

1 teaspoon salt

1 teaspoon freshly ground black pepper

¹/₃ cup Madeira

1 teaspoon freshly squeezed lemon juice

6 ounces goat cheese, crumbled

1 tablespoon minced fresh parsley

1 pound phyllo dough

¹/₂ cup melted butter

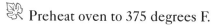 Preheat oven to 375 degrees F.

In a skillet, melt the ¹/₄ cup of butter over medium heat. Add the shallots and sauté until tender. Add the mushrooms and sauté until lightly browned.

*(recipe continued on next page)*

Add the chicken stock, thyme, salt, and pepper and simmer until the liquid has almost evaporated. Stir in the Madeira and the lemon juice and simmer until the liquid has almost evaporated. Remove from the heat and stir in the goat cheese and parsley. Let cool.

Unfold the phyllo sheets. Use only 1 sheet at a time and keep the remaining sheets covered with a damp tea towel to prevent them from drying out. Lay one sheet on a cutting board. Using a pastry brush, brush the phyllo with melted butter. Lay a second sheet on top of the first, and brush with butter. Continue layering and buttering until you have used 4 sheets of the phyllo. Using a sharp knife, cut the phyllo lengthwise into 3 strips. Place 1 heaping tablespoon of the filling at the center of the bottom of one strip. Fold one corner over to form a triangle. Continue folding over the triangle to the end of the strip. Brush top with butter and place on a baking sheet. Repeat until all the phyllo and the filling are used. Bake for 12 to 15 minutes or until golden brown. Serve warm.

*Makes about 24*
*Serve with Kenwood Vineyards and Winery*
*Chardonnay*

58

## LEDSON VINEYARDS
## AND WINERY

*One of Northern California's newest wineries, Ledson is rapidly making a name for itself with its reserve Merlots, floral and fruity Rieslings, and intense Chardonnays. Located in Sonoma County's Valley of the Moon, Ledson is at home in a fantastic brick-and-mortar Gothic-style mansion known affectionately as "The Castle." Two full-time chefs guarantee Ledson's commitment to the art and culture of pairing food and great wine.*

# PUMPKIN BREAD
## *in a Jar*

*Since this pumpkin bread is baked in its own
container, it is perfect to take along on a picnic
or to give as a gift.*

1 cup pumpkin purée

$1/2$ cup vegetable oil

$1/2$ cup water

2 eggs

1 cup granulated sugar

$1/2$ cup brown sugar

$12/3$ cups all-purpose flour

1 teaspoon baking soda

1 teaspoon cinnamon

$3/4$ teaspoon salt

$1/2$ teaspoon allspice

$1/2$ teaspoon ground cloves

$1/4$ teaspoon baking powder

$1/2$ cup chopped walnuts

Preheat oven to 350 degrees F. Lightly oil 4 wide-mouth pint canning jars.

In a large bowl, combine the pumpkin purée, oil, water, and eggs and beat until smooth. Add the granulated sugar and brown sugar and beat until smooth. In a separate bowl, sift together the flour, baking soda, cinnamon, salt, allspice, cloves, and baking powder. Add to the pumpkin mixture and beat until smooth. Stir in the walnuts.

Divide the batter evenly into the canning jars. Place the jars on a baking sheet and place in the oven. Bake for 40 minutes. Remove the canning jars from the oven and cool completely. The pumpkin bread will rise slightly above the tops of the canning jars while baking, but will shrink when cool. Cover each jar with a lid.

*Makes 4 loaves*
*Serve with Ledson Vineyards and Winery Johannisberg Riesling*

## LOUIS MARTINI

*Louis Martini wines are made in the classic tradition, to accompany food, to enhance its flavor, and to celebrate the sharing of mealtime among family and friends. The Martinis have always made wines that they drink themselves, in the belief that others will take pleasure in them as well. They say their wines are not made to win awards, although they win acclaim time and time again. They say their wines are not made to be museum pieces, although they have made history with their pioneering winemaking techniques. They say their wines are made simply to enjoy. Since they first settled in the Napa Valley over 60 years ago, the Martinis have been part of the history of Northern California winemaking, and their commitment to the vine is evident to all who visit the winery or taste their wines.*

# SESAME CHICKEN WINGS

*Baked to a rich, golden brown, these juicy wings will fill your kitchen with the fragrance of ginger and toasted sesame seeds. Definitely finger food!*

2 pounds chicken wings

1/2 cup minced scallions

1/3 cup soy sauce

1/4 cup dry sherry

1 tablespoon brown sugar

1 tablespoon sesame oil

2 teaspoons minced fresh ginger

1 clove garlic, minced

2 tablespoons chopped cilantro

2 tablespoons sesame seeds, lightly toasted

*(recipe continued on next page)*

🍂 Preheat oven to 425 degrees F. Lightly oil a
9 x 13-inch baking dish.

Place the chicken wings into the prepared baking dish. In a bowl, whisk together the scallions, soy sauce, sherry, brown sugar, sesame oil, ginger, and garlic and pour over the chicken. Bake for about 1 hour, or until the chicken wings are a deep golden brown and almost all of the liquid has evaporated. Transfer the chicken wings to a platter and sprinkle with cilantro and sesame seeds.

*Serves 4*
*Serve with Louis Martini*
*Zinfandel*

*A man will be eloquent if you give him good wine.*

**Ralph Waldo Emerson**

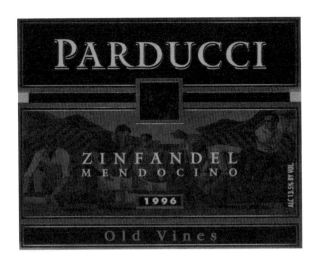

## PARDUCCI WINE ESTATES

*There are only two things you need to know about a wine. First, do you like it? Second, can you afford it? The people at Parducci are confident that, after tasting and pricing Parducci wines, the answer to both questions will be an emphatic "Yes!" They have always recognized that wine customers enjoy a variety of wines. As such, they have taken advantage of the numerous varieties grown in Mendocino County and produce all the following: Cabernet Sauvignon, Chenin Blanc, Pinot Noir, Chardonnay, Charbono, Barbera, Petite Sirah, Merlot, Sauvignon Blanc, Zinfandel, Syrah, and Sangiovese. Parducci strives to bring out the varietal characteristics each grape has to offer, and believes that wine is an honest, natural product that should never be over-processed. It should have a softness that invites pleasant consumption upon release.*

# PANZANELLA
## *(Tomato & Bread Salad)*

*This is an excellent cold summer salad.*

**DRESSING:**

1/4 cup balsamic vinegar

3 shallots, minced

2 cloves garlic, minced

2 tablespoons minced fresh parsley

2 teaspoons minced fresh oregano

1 teaspoon salt

1/2 teaspoon freshly ground white pepper

1/2 cup olive oil

6 thick slices stale sourdough bread, cubed
   and lightly toasted

6 tomatoes, seeded and cut into 1-inch pieces

**For the dressing:** In a bowl, whisk together the vinegar, shallots, garlic, parsley, oregano, salt, and white pepper until the salt dissolves. Whisk in the olive oil and set aside.

In a large bowl, combine the bread and tomatoes. Pour the dressing over the bread and tomatoes and toss together. Cover and chill 1 hour in the refrigerator, tossing occasionally, to allow the bread to absorb the dressing.

*Serves 6*
*Serve with Parducci Wine Estates*
*Zinfandel*

## MINER FAMILY
## VINEYARDS

*Located on the Silverado Trail in a new and modern winery, Miner Family Vineyards produces inky, dark Cabernets and Merlots, as well as complex and balanced Chardonnays from their estate vineyards high up in the eastern hills of the Oakville appellation of the Napa Valley. Low yields from the ancient, rocky volcanic soil serve to amplify and intensify the structure of these classic Napa Valley wines. Additionally, small lots of Sauvignon Blanc, Viognier, Pinot Noir, Zinfandel, Syrah, and Sangiovese are available in limited quantities.*

# TABBOULEH

*Susan Bishop serves this tabbouleh stuffed into pita bread or as a side dish with grilled lamb kebabs.*

1 1/2 cups cracked bulgur wheat

4 tomatoes, peeled, seeded, and chopped

1 English cucumber, peeled, seeded, and diced

6 scallions, chopped

1/2 cup pitted Greek olives, sliced

1/4 cup finely chopped fresh mint

1/2 cup olive oil

Juice of 4 lemons

2 teaspoons salt

1 teaspoon freshly ground black pepper

Place the bulgur in a large bowl. Add enough hot water to cover the bulgur and let stand for 40 minutes. Drain the bulgur through a sieve. Return the bulgur to the bowl. Add the tomatoes, cucumber, scallions, olives, and mint and toss gently to mix.

In a small bowl, stir together the olive oil, lemon juice, salt, and pepper. Pour over the bulgur mixture and toss lightly to mix. Cover and chill overnight.

*Serves 8*
*Serve with Miner Family Vineyards*
*Zinfandel*

# MUMM CUVÉE NAPA

*Journey through the vineyards, along the peaceful Silverado Trail, to the glorious home of Mumm Cuvée Napa. Imagine yourself on a terrace, seated under the cool shade of an elegant umbrella. The sun is setting over the Mayacamas Mountains in the distance, with soft amber and purple hues settling over the hills and vineyards. These images are reflected in your hand by a flute of America's finest sparkling wine—Mumm Cuvée Napa.*

# SPICY MARINATED OLIVES

*These olives are excellent finger food, either on a summer picnic or as an hors d'oeuvre at home.*

1/2 cup olive oil

1/2 cup balsamic vinegar

3 sprigs fresh rosemary, each 6 inches long

4 sprigs fresh thyme, each 3 inches long

4 cloves garlic, cut in half

1 teaspoon pickling spice

1 teaspoon hot red chile flakes

3 bay leaves

10 whole peppercorns

3 cups Kalamata olives, rinsed and drained

In a 1-quart jar with a tight-fitting lid, combine the olive oil, balsamic vinegar, rosemary, thyme, garlic, pickling spice, red chile flakes, bay leaves, and peppercorns. Cover the jar and shake to mix the marinade. Add the olives and cover the jar tightly. Chill for 10 days in the refrigerator, turning the jar upside down every day.

*Makes 3 cups*
*Serve with Mumm Cuvée Napa*
*Brut Prestige*

## PEJU PROVINCE

Peju Province is one of the few family-owned and operated wineries in the Napa Valley. The winery's thirty acres of quality vineyards are located in the famed Rutherford bench, Napa's renowned Cabernet region. In addition to Cabernet Sauvignon, Chardonnay, Merlot, and Cabernet Franc, Peju Province produces small lots of unusual wines such as their Carnival, Provence, and Late Harvest. The winery's long-term commitment to quality has won accolades from many in the wine trade, and their wines are sought after by a growing cadre of wine lovers and aficionados.

# CAPELLINI SALAD

*Herta Peju's capellini salad tastes especially wonderful when served at a sunny summery picnic.*

¹/4 cup olive oil

2 tablespoons balsamic vinegar

1 teaspoon minced jalapeño chile

¹/2 teaspoon minced fresh ginger

Salt and freshly ground black pepper to taste

6 ounces capellini pasta, cooked in boiling salted water until al dente, then drained

1 carrot, julienned

1 small red onion, thinly sliced

1 red bell pepper, julienned

1 zucchini, julienned

¹/4 cup pine nuts, lightly toasted

In a large bowl, whisk together the olive oil, balsamic vinegar, jalapeño chile, ginger, salt, and pepper. Add the hot pasta and toss to coat. Add the carrot, red onion, bell pepper, zucchini, and pine nuts and toss to coat. Cover and chill overnight, tossing occasionally to distribute the dressing.

*Serves 6*
*Serve with Peju Province*
*Chardonnay*

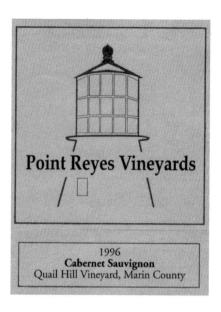

1996
**Cabernet Sauvignon**
Quail Hill Vineyard, Marin County

# POINT REYES
# VINEYARDS

*Point Reyes Vineyards is a family-owned operation situated on scenic Highway 1, overlooking the beautiful Point Reyes National Seashore, 40 miles north of San Francisco. For three generations, the Doughty family has proudly farmed the rich, fertile lands of Marin County. In 1990, their love of fine wines led to the planting of a small vineyard. They knew that the quality of Marin County's soil and the diversity of its microclimates would provide the perfect conditions to grow grapes for ultra-premium wines. The vineyard's success resulted in wines that are rich, well-rounded, complex and full of unique flavors. The Doughty family opened the first commercial wine-tasting room in Marin since the 1930s. They invite you to enjoy what is truly the fruits of their labor.*

# HOME-SMOKED SALMON

*The brine used for this excellent smoked salmon also works quite well with sturgeon or trout.*

1 cup brown sugar

1 cup Point Reyes Vineyards Sparkling Wine

1 cup soy sauce

1 cup water

1/4 cup non-iodized salt

1/2 teaspoon garlic powder

1/2 teaspoon onion powder

1/2 teaspoon freshly ground black pepper

1/2 teaspoon Tabasco sauce

3 1/2 pounds boneless, skinless salmon fillet, cut into 4 pieces

3 cups hickory, alder, or cherry chips, soaked in water for 1 hour

*(recipe continued on next page)*

In a large stainless steel or glass bowl, combine the brown sugar, wine, soy sauce, water, salt, garlic powder, onion powder, pepper, and Tabasco sauce. Stir until the sugar and salt dissolve. Place the salmon pieces in the brine and weigh down with a plate. Cover with plastic wrap and refrigerate for 24 hours.

Remove the salmon from the brine and rinse lightly. Place the salmon on a rack and allow to air-dry for 1 hour.

Drain the hickory, alder, or cherry chips and place in a smoker. Place the salmon in the smoker and smoke according to manufacturer's directions for 8 to 10 hours, depending on the thickness of the fillets.

*Serves 4*
*Serve with Point Reyes Vineyards*
*Cabernet Sauvignon*

## RMS ALAMBIC DISTILLERY

*Located among the rolling hillsides of the Carneros region of the Napa Valley, RMS Distillery practices traditional methods of brandy distillation. Six different varieties of grapes are double distilled in classic Alambic pot stills imported from Cognac. The classic Cognac method of distilling on the lees captures the essence of the ripe California fruit and maximizes the complexity of their fine brandies. Extended aging in French Limousin Oak barrels imparts toasty spice and rich vanilla flavors.*

# BRANDIED BISCOTTI

*These deliciously different biscotti keep well and are ideal as a "take-along" for your next trip.*

$^2/3$ cup finely chopped dried apricots

$^2/3$ cup finely chopped sun-dried cherries

$^2/3$ cup finely chopped golden raisins

$^1/4$ cup RMS Alambic Distillery Special Reserve Brandy

$^1/2$ cup butter, softened

$1^1/4$ cups sugar

$2^1/2$ teaspoons baking powder

$^1/4$ teaspoon salt

3 eggs

$1^1/2$ teaspoons vanilla extract

$^1/2$ teaspoon almond extract

3 cups all-purpose flour

$^1/2$ cup lightly toasted hazelnuts, finely chopped

$^1/2$ cup shelled pistachio nuts, finely chopped

In a bowl, stir together the apricots, cherries, raisins, and brandy. Cover and let stand overnight at room temperature.

Preheat oven to 375 degrees F.

In a large bowl, beat the butter for 30 seconds. Add the sugar, baking powder, and salt and beat until smooth. Add the eggs, vanilla extract, and almond extract and beat until smooth. Add the flour and beat until smooth. Stir in the hazelnuts, the pistachios, and the reserved dried fruits and their liquid.

Divide the dough into 2 portions and turn out onto a floured surface. Lightly flour your hands because the dough will be sticky, and shape the dough into logs. Place the dough logs on a baking sheet. Bake for 25 to 30 minutes, or until light golden brown. Remove from the oven and slice crosswise about 1 inch thick. Place slices, cut-side up, on baking sheets and return to the oven. Bake for 15 to 20 minutes more, or until the biscotti are crisp and dry. Cool on a rack.

*Makes about 3 dozen*
*Serve with RMS Alambic Distillery*
*Special Reserve Brandy*

1996

ROBERT MONDAVI

NAPA VALLEY

PINOT NOIR

ALCOHOL 13.5% BY VOLUME

## ROBERT MONDAVI WINERY

*Founded in 1966 by Robert Mondavi and his son, Michael, the Robert Mondavi Winery is considered a leader in the modern wine industry. They are committed to producing naturally balanced wines of great finesse and elegance that complement and enhance fine food. They have been successful in achieving these goals through earth-friendly farming practices, a sophisticated winery emphasizing gentle treatment of their wines, and a genuine love for their handiwork. No other winery epitomizes the Napa Valley like the Robert Mondavi Winery.*

# ITALIAN TORTA

*This layered savory torta is jam-packed with the finest delicacies. Serve cold with a glass of Robert Mondavi's Pinot Noir.*

### DOUGH:

1 cup warm water

1 package active dry yeast

1 tablespoon sugar

$1/2$ teaspoon salt

3 to $3^1/2$ cups bread flour

### FILLING:

1 package (10-ounces) frozen spinach, thawed and squeezed dry

1 cup ricotta cheese

6 ounces prosciutto, chopped

1 egg, lightly beaten

2 cloves garlic, minced

8 ounces salami, thinly sliced

1 can (14-ounces) artichoke bottoms in brine, drained and chopped

8 ounces provolone cheese, thinly sliced

$1/2$ cup finely chopped Kalamata olives

1 egg

1 teaspoon water

*(recipe continued on next page)*

For the dough: In a large bowl, stir together the warm water, yeast, and sugar. Let the mixture stand until foamy. Stir in the salt. Stir in 3 cups of the bread flour until it is all absorbed. If necessary, stir in enough of the remaining bread flour to form a stiff dough. Turn the dough out onto a lightly floured surface and knead until the dough is smooth and satiny, about 10 minutes. Place the dough in a lightly oiled bowl and turn to coat. Cover with a damp tea towel and let rise in a warm spot until doubled in size, about $1^{1}/2$ hours.

Punch the dough down and knead a few times on a lightly floured surface. Cut off one-fourth of the dough and roll out into a 10-inch circle. Set aside. Roll out the remaining dough to fit a 10-inch springform pan, with 1 inch of the dough hanging over the edge.

For the filling: In a large bowl, stir together the spinach, ricotta cheese, prosciutto, beaten egg, and garlic until well combined. Spread the mixture into the bottom of the dough-lined springform pan. Arrange half of the salami over the spinach mixture. Sprinkle the artichoke bottoms evenly over the salami. Arrange half of the provolone cheese over the artichoke bottoms. Bring up the sides of the excess dough and fold over the filling, pinching to seal. Sprinkle the chopped olives on the middle of the dough leaving a 1-inch border. Arrange the remaining salami on top of the olives. Arrange the remaining provolone cheese on top of the salami. In a small bowl, whisk together the egg and 1 teaspoon of water to make an egg wash. Brush the egg wash on the edge of the dough. Fit the reserved circle of dough over the top of the provolone and seal the edges together. Brush the top with the egg wash and prick the dough several times decoratively with a fork. Let the dough rise for 15 minutes.

Preheat oven to 350 degrees F.

Bake the torta for 50 to 60 minutes, or until the top is golden brown. Remove the torta from the oven and let cool completely in the springform pan. Remove the sides of the springform pan. Slice into wedges with a serrated knife and serve at room temperature.

*Serves 6 to 8*
*Serve with Robert Mondavi Winery*
*Pinot Noir*

## RODNEY STRONG
## VINEYARDS

*Over 35 years ago Rodney Strong was one of the first to recognize Sonoma County's potential for excellence. After searching for vineyard land that would bring each grape variety to its fullest potential, Rodney Strong finally selected vineyard sites in the Chalk Hill, Alexander Valley, and Russian River Valley appellations to produce his wine. In the cellar, he employs the subtle use of barrel and stainless steel fermentation, oak aging, and other winemaking techniques to bring out the best in the fruit. All this is in keeping with his philosophy to allow the grapes from each vineyard to express their individual character in the final bottled wine.*

# OLIVITA

*This intensely delicious olive spread is best when served atop a slice of rustic country bread.*

8 ounces Kalamata olives, pitted

2 tablespoons olive oil

2 teaspoons freshly squeezed lemon juice

2 cloves garlic, minced

$^1/_2$ teaspoon oregano

Freshly ground white pepper to taste

1 baguette, thinly sliced

In the bowl of a food processor, combine the olives, olive oil, lemon juice, garlic, oregano, and white pepper. Process until the olives are finely chopped, scraping the sides of the bowl frequently. Cover and chill in the refrigerator for 2 hours before serving, to allow the flavors to marry. Serve with the baguette slices.

*Makes about 1 cup*
*Serve with Rodney Strong Vineyards*
*Pinot Noir*

## SCHWEIGER VINEYARDS
## AND WINERY

*Fred and Sally Schweiger have turned their estate winery into one of the most picturesque properties in the Napa Valley. Located high above St. Helena, atop Spring Mountain, their vines have found ideal growing conditions within the volcanic ash soils of this section of the Mayacamas mountain range. Chardonnay, Merlot, and Cabernet Sauvignon are the three varieties upon which the Schweigers have built their reputation. Opulent with fruit, the red wines exhibit firm tannins and fine structure, while their Chardonnay astounds with supple mouth-filling elegance.*

# COLD POACHED SALMON *with Cilantro Pesto Aioli*

*Sally Schweiger serves this elegant salmon with thin slices of French bread.*

3 pounds salmon fillet, skinned and all bones removed

**COURT BOUILLON:**

6 cups water

1 cup Schweiger Vineyards and Winery Chardonnay

1 onion, peeled

1/4 cup chopped carrot

1/4 cup chopped celery

1 bay leaf

4 whole cloves

1 teaspoon salt

1/4 teaspoon freshly ground black pepper

**CILANTRO PESTO AIOLI:**

1 bunch cilantro, leaves only

2 cloves garlic, minced

1 1/2 cups mayonnaise

*(recipe continued on next page)*

🌿 Preheat oven to 350 degrees F.

Place the salmon fillet in a baking dish just large enough to hold the salmon. Set aside.

**For the court bouillon:** In a large pot, combine the water, wine, onion, carrot, celery, bay leaf, cloves, salt, and pepper. Bring to a boil, then reduce the heat to medium and simmer for 15 minutes. Strain the bouillon through a sieve and discard the solids. Pour the hot court bouillon over the salmon, making sure that the fillet is covered with the poaching liquid. Place in the oven for 20 minutes. Remove from the oven and let the salmon cool in the poaching liquid. Cover and chill in the poaching liquid for 6 hours.

**For the aioli:** In the bowl of a food processor, combine the cilantro and garlic and pulse until smooth, scraping the sides often. Add the mayonnaise and pulse until smooth. Transfer to a small serving dish, cover and chill for at least 1 hour to allow flavors to marry.

Drain off the poaching liquid and serve the salmon cold with the aioli.

*Serves 8*
*Serve with Schweiger Vineyards and Winery*
*Chardonnay*

## SONOMA-CUTRER
## VINEYARDS

*Founded in January 1973 by Brice Cutrer Jones and Kent Klineman, Sonoma-Cutrer has focused on the production of outstanding Chardonnay from its vineyards in the Sonoma Coast viticultural appellation. To achieve their goal of producing the highest quality wine, they have selected hillside and rocky soils and planted them with the newest high-quality Dijon clones of Chardonnay. They are densely planted on low-vigor rootstocks and are trellised in traditional Burgundian fashion. Extended underground aging of the wines in proprietary French oak barrels produces wines of distinction and character.*

# PISTACHIO-PAPRIKA
# CHICKEN SALAD
## *with Lemon Cream Dressing*

*Serve with a large loaf of crusted French bread.*

### LEMON CREAM DRESSING:

1/2 cup heavy cream

1 1/2 tablespoons freshly squeezed lemon juice

1 teaspoon Dijon mustard

1 teaspoon salt

3/4 teaspoon freshly ground black pepper

3 tablespoons olive oil


2 cups diced cooked chicken breasts

4 cups baby spinach

2 tablespoons olive oil

1 1/2 tablespoons fresh squeezed lemon juice

1/2 cup shelled pistachio nuts, lightly toasted
and chopped

1 teaspoon paprika

**For the dressing:** In a bowl, whisk together the cream, lemon juice, Dijon mustard, salt, and pepper until the salt has dissolved. Whisk in the olive oil. Add the chicken to the dressing and toss to coat.

In a large bowl, combine the spinach, olive oil, and lemon juice and toss to coat. Divide the spinach onto 4 plates and top with the chicken. Sprinkle with pistachio nuts and paprika.

*Serves 4*
*Serve with Sonoma-Cutrer Vineyards*
*Chardonnay*

*Where there is no wine there is no love.*

Euripedes

## ST. SUPÉRY VINEYARDS AND WINERY

*No visit to the Napa Valley would be complete without a visit to the St. Supéry Wine Discovery Center in Rutherford. A demonstration vineyard, galleries within the center filled with panoramic murals, and displays all illustrate the lore of the vine. Both self-guided and guided tours serve to introduce the visitor to the wines and philosophy of St. Supéry.*

# CRISP & TANGY LEMON CHICKEN

*Removing the skin of the chicken eliminates about half the fat. Executive chef Sunny Cristadoro devised this lemony yogurt marinade to replace fat with flavor.*

$1/2$ cup nonfat yogurt

1 tablespoon minced fresh ginger

4 cloves garlic, minced

2 teaspoons cumin

2 teaspoons freshly squeezed lemon juice

2 teaspoons soy sauce

1 teaspoon coriander

1 teaspoon freshly ground black pepper

1 teaspoon tumeric

4 whole chicken legs, skin removed

2 cups dried bread crumbs

*(recipe continued on next page)*

In a bowl, whisk together the yogurt, ginger, garlic, cumin, lemon juice, soy sauce, coriander, pepper, and tumeric. Place the chicken in a shallow dish large enough to hold the chicken legs in a single layer. Coat the chicken with the yogurt mixture. Cover and chill overnight.

Preheat oven to 375 degrees F. Place a rack inside a rimmed baking sheet.

Place the bread crumbs in a shallow dish. Remove the chicken legs from the marinade. Coat the chicken with the bread crumbs on all sides. Place the chicken on the rack. Bake for 45 to 55 minutes, or until the juices run clear when the chicken is pierced with a skewer.

*Serves 4*
*Serve with St. Supéry Vineyards and Winery Sauvignon Blanc*

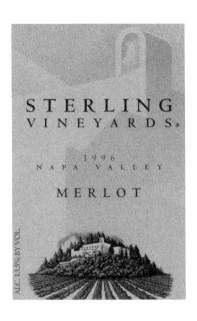

## STERLING
## VINEYARDS

*Built in the architectural style of the Greek island of Mykonos, the Sterling Vineyards winery sits dramatically atop a 300-foot knoll just south of Napa Valley's northernmost town, Calistoga. Its white, monastic buildings contrast sharply with the dark green trees that cover the knoll. Visitors are carried up to the winery by aerial tramway and treated to a spectacular view of the Napa Valley below, as well as a close-up look at the Napa Valley's most dramatic and recognizable winery. The panorama is awe-inspiring and peaceful, punctuated only by the peal of Sterling's antique English church bells.*

# CARAMELIZED ONION, PROSCIUTTO & BRIE
## *in Puff Pastry*

*These savory pastries, from my dear friend Judie Vacchina, are perfect to tuck into your picnic basket.*

2 tablespoons butter

4 onions, finely chopped

1 tablespoon water

1 teaspoon sugar

1 tablespoon olive oil

8 ounces prosciutto, finely diced

8 ounces Brie cheese

1 pound puff pastry

Preheat oven to 375 degrees F. Lightly oil a baking sheet.

In a large skillet, melt the butter over medium heat. Add the onions, water, and sugar. Reduce the heat to medium-low, cover, and cook for 45 minutes, or until the mixture is very thick and a deep golden brown. Stir occasionally and add a little water if the onions begin to scorch. Remove from the heat and let cool.

In a skillet, heat the olive oil over medium heat. Add prosciutto and sauté until lightly crispy. Remove from the heat and let cool.

Cut the rind off the Brie cheese and discard. Finely dice the cheese and set aside.

Roll out the puff pastry to an 8 x 14-inch rectangle. Spread the caramelized onions evenly over the puff pastry. Sprinkle the prosciutto and Brie evenly over the caramelized onions. Roll up jelly-roll fashion and place on prepared baking sheet. Chill in the refrigerator for 30 minutes.

Transfer to a cutting board and slice into $3/4$-inch slices. Place the slices on the prepared baking sheet and bake for about 20 minutes, or until golden brown. Serve hot or at room temperature.

*Makes 18*
*Serve with Sterling Vineyards*
*Merlot*

## STONE CREEK
## WINERY

*Stone Creek's Tasting Room is located in Kenwood in the heart of Sonoma County, in what was once a one-room schoolhouse. This historical building was erected in 1890 and was one of the first public schools in the Los Guilicos Valley. In addition to its colorful history, the "Old Blue Schoolhouse" is now the home of Stone Creek Wines.*

# CURED SALMON
## *with Honey Dijon Sauce*

*Marc Downie, from Catering by Design, serves his divine salmon over fresh mixed greens with crusty bread.*

### CURED SALMON:

2$^1$/$_2$ pounds salmon fillet, all bones removed

1$^1$/$_2$ cups sugar

$^1$/$_2$ cup non-iodized salt

$^1$/$_4$ cup fennel seeds, crushed

1 bunch fresh dill, chopped

### HONEY DIJON SAUCE:

$^1$/$_4$ cup honey

$^1$/$_4$ cup Dijon mustard

White pepper to taste

1 pound mixed baby greens

*(recipe continued on next page)*

🐚 **For the salmon:** Place the salmon fillet, skin side down, in a 9 x 13-inch glass baking dish. In a small bowl, stir together the sugar and salt with a fork until blended. Cover the salmon evenly with the mixture. Sprinkle the fennel seed over the sugar mixture. Sprinkle the dill evenly over the top. Press the dill firmly onto the salmon. Using a fork, pierce through the salmon until the fork touches the baking dish. Continue to pierce the salmon all over. Cover the baking dish completely with plastic wrap. Place a smaller baking dish on top of the salmon and place several heavy weights, such as canned goods, in the smaller baking dish. This will help extract the liquid from the salmon during the curing. Place in the refrigerator for 3 days. Once every day pour off the accumulated liquid from the salmon. On the 4th day, remove the salmon and rinse off the curing spices.

**For the sauce:** In a small bowl, whisk together the honey, Dijon mustard, and white pepper. Cover and chill for 1 hour to allow flavors to marry.

Grill or bake the salmon just until the meat flakes. Serve over mixed greens and drizzle with the sauce.

*Serves 8 to 10*
*Serve with Stone Creek Winery*
*Zinfandel*

## TOAD HOLLOW
## VINEYARDS

*Todd Williams (Dr. Toad) and his reclusive winemaker, known only as the dancing badger on Toad Hollow's label, have fashioned Toad Hollow with a commitment to producing the highest quality wine at the most affordable price. They purposefully choose not to age their Chardonnay in oak, preferring instead to maintain the delicate fruit of their grapes by cool-fermenting in 100% stainless steel. After yeast and subsequent malolactic fermentation, their wines are fruity and refreshing, without the distraction of big, bold wood. Toadmaster Todd also produces a delicate rosé from a blend of Pinot Noir and Petite Sirah. Their name for it? What else but "Eye of the Toad." When asked about his wine priorities, Dr. Toad summarizes them succinctly: "Enjoy it with pleasure, enjoy it often, and don't make a big deal out of it."*

# THRESHER SHARK
## *with Spicy Salsa*

*Enjoy this hot and spicy fish on a warm summer evening with a cold bottle of Toad Hollow's Chardonnay and some special friends.*

SPICY SALSA:

3 Roma tomatoes, seeded and chopped

1 small red onion, finely chopped

1 small red bell pepper, finely chopped

1 avocado, diced

1 can (4-ounces) green chiles, minced

2 cloves garlic, minced

Juice of 2 limes

1/2 teaspoon Tabasco sauce

Salt and freshly ground black pepper to taste


Juice of 2 limes

Salt and freshly ground black pepper to taste

4 thresher shark steaks, 5 ounces each

**For the salsa:** In a bowl, combine the tomatoes, red onion, bell pepper, avocado, chiles, garlic, lime juice, Tabasco, salt, and pepper and toss gently to mix. Cover and let stand at room temperature for 1 hour to allow the flavors to marry.

In a dish large enough to hold the fish in a single layer, whisk together the lime juice, salt, and pepper. Place the shark steaks in the marinade and turn to coat. Cover and chill for 30 minutes.

Prepare the grill. Remove the shark from the marinade and pat dry. Season with salt and pepper. Grill about 4 to 5 minutes per side, or until the fish just starts to flake. Do not overcook. Serve topped with a dollop of salsa.

*Serves 4*
*Serve with Toad Hollow Vineyards*
*Chardonnay*

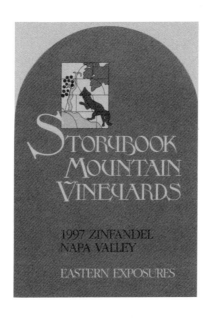

## STORYBOOK MOUNTAIN VINEYARDS

*At the extreme northern end of the Napa Valley lies Storybook Mountain Vineyards. Storybook Mountain is totally dedicated to Zinfandel and has established a worldwide reputation for consistently high quality. Proprietors Jerry and Sigrid Seps age their Zinfandel a minimum of twelve months inside century-old caves dug deep into the volcanic rock underlying their vineyards. Their wines are famed for their elegance and longevity. Notes of raspberries, black cherries, and spice are the keynote of these complex, well-balanced wines.*

# GOLDEN
# NUGGETS

*These charming treats would be part of a
delectable antipasto selection.*

1 1/2 cups all-purpose flour

1 teaspoon paprika

8 ounces sharp cheddar cheese, finely grated

1/2 cup butter, softened

40 to 45 pimiento stuffed green olives, drained

Preheat oven to 400 degrees F.

In a large bowl, stir together the flour and
paprika until blended. Add the cheese and butter
and blend into a smooth dough. Roll 2 teaspoons of
the dough into a ball. Flatten into a disk. Wrap the
dough around an olive, enclosing it completely, and
seal the dough. Place on a baking sheet. Repeat
until all of the dough and olives are used.

Bake for about 20 minutes, or until golden
brown. Serve warm or at room temperature.

*Makes about 40 to 45*
*Serve with Storybook Mountain Vineyards*
*    Zinfandel*

## TREFETHEN VINEYARDS

*Tradition combines with technology at Trefethen Vineyards, where a century-old winery and the latest in winemaking equipment give the Trefethen family, and their wines, the best of both worlds. First planted to grapes in the 1850s, the Eshcol ranch, as it was known back then, received its name from a biblical allusion to an immense cluster of grapes. In 1968, Gene and Katie Trefethen revitalized the old Eshcol property and planted new vines on the 600-acre valley estate and on 50 acres to the northwest. The first wines were vinified in 1973, and today wine production has climbed to 75,000 cases per year. The Trefethen family has this to say about their wines: "Winemaking is part agriculture and part parenting. We are proud to introduce you to what we have worried over and cared for—our wines. They are meant to be shared and enjoyed among friends."*

# CHILLED ROASTED CORN & GREEN BEAN SOUP

*Janet Trefethen has given us her special cold summer soup to enjoy on a hot summer day.*

8 ears of corn in the husks

3 cups chicken stock or vegetable stock

Salt and freshly ground black pepper to taste

8 ounces green beans

3 tablespoons water

Fresh chervil sprigs for garnish

 Prepare a medium-hot fire in the grill. Grill the corn in their husks until the husks are browned on all sides. Remove from the grill and let cool.

Remove the husks and corn silk and cut off the kernels. In a large pot, combine the corn kernals and chicken or vegetable stock. Bring to a boil, cover, then reduce heat to low and simmer for 20 minutes, or until the corn is very tender. With a slotted spoon, remove 1 cup of the corn kernels and reserve. Purée the remaining corn and liquid in a blender. Strain through a fine sieve, pressing down on the solids. Stir in the reserved corn kernels. Let cool, then

*(recipe continued on next page)*

season with salt and pepper. Cover and chill for 6 hours in the refrigerator.

Bring a large pot of salted water to a boil. Add the beans and cook and until tender, about 7 minutes. Drain, then rinse under cold water. Purée the beans with 3 tablespoons water in a blender until smooth. Cover and chill for 6 hours.

Ladle the corn soup into mugs or bowls. Place a dollop of the green bean purée in the center of the soup. Pull a knife tip through the purée to create a design. Garnish with the chervil sprigs. Serve cold.

*Serves 6*
*Serve with Trefethen Vineyards*
*Chardonnay*

*A bottle of wine begs to be shared;*
*I have never met a miserly wine lover.*

**Clifton Fadiman**

## V. SATTUI WINERY

*V. Sattui Winery is a family-owned winery established in 1885 and located in St. Helena, the very heart of California's famous Napa Valley. Their award-winning wines are sold exclusively at the winery, by mail order, and from their website direct to customers. Surrounding the beautiful stone winery is a large tree-shaded picnic ground. V. Sattui also boasts a large gourmet cheese shop and deli.*

# CHINESE CHICKEN SALAD *with Cashews*

*Cold salads are a perfect no-muss, no-fuss picnic treat.*

**DRESSING:**

1/4 cup vegetable oil

3 tablespoons sesame oil

2 tablespoons orange juice

2 tablespoons rice vinegar

2 tablespoons soy sauce

2 teaspoons mirin

1 teaspoon minced fresh ginger

1 teaspoon sugar

1 clove garlic, minced

1/4 teaspoon hot red chile flakes

1/4 teaspoon salt

1/4 teaspoon freshly ground black pepper

4 cups finely shredded cabbage

2 cups diced cooked chicken

1/2 cup cashew nuts, coarsely chopped

1/3 cup finely diced red bell pepper

2 scallions, chopped

1 tablespoon finely chopped chives

**For the dressing:** In a large bowl, whisk together the vegetable oil, sesame oil, orange juice, rice vinegar, soy sauce, mirin, ginger, sugar, garlic, red chile flakes, salt, and pepper until the sugar and salt dissolve.

Add the cabbage, chicken, cashews, bell pepper, scallions, and chives and toss to mix well. Cover and chill for at least 1 hour in the refrigerator, tossing occasionally, to allow the flavors to marry.

*Serves 4*
*Serve with V. Sattui Winery*
*Chardonnay*

*Chardonnay*

## VALLEY OF THE MOON
## WINERY AND VINEYARDS

*Embracing the traditions of one of the world's most famous winegrowing areas, Sonoma County, the creation of the Valley of the Moon wines begins with hand selecting the absolute highest-quality fruit available from their organically farmed estate vineyards and those of a select few growers in Sonoma. The winery's vineyards are planted to the well-drained, rocky, red volcanic soil characteristic of the southern Sonoma Valley. The vineyards enjoy a banana belt-type microclimate, producing traditional varietals that include old-vine Zinfandel, Syrah, and Sangiovese grapes with intense colors and flavors.*

# ARTICHOKE & PANCETTA QUICHE
## *with Macadamia Crust*

*This savory quiche from Linda Kittler is a perfect pairing for the Valley of the Moon Chardonnay.*

MACADAMIA CRUST:

1$^1$/2 cups all-purpose flour

1 teaspoon thyme

$^1$/2 teaspoon freshly ground black pepper

$^1$/2 teaspoon salt

$^3$/4 cup cold butter, cut into small pieces

$^1$/2 cup finely chopped macadamia nuts

$^1$/4 cup cold water

*(recipe continued on next page)*

## ARTICHOKE AND PANCETTA FILLING:

1$^1$/$_2$ cups half-and-half

3 eggs

$^1$/$_4$ teaspoon freshly ground black pepper

$^1$/$_4$ teaspoon salt

$^1$/$_4$ teaspoon thyme

2 tablespoons butter

2 tablespoons olive oil

6 ounces pancetta, chopped

1 cup thinly sliced leeks, white and pale green
   parts only

1 can (14-ounces) artichoke bottoms in brine,
   coarsely chopped

1 cup grated Monterey jack cheese

2 tablespoons freshly grated Asiago cheese

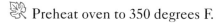 Preheat oven to 350 degrees F.

**For the crust:** In a large bowl, stir together
the flour, thyme, pepper, and salt. Cut in the butter pieces until mixture resembles coarse meal.
Stir in the macadamia nuts. Sprinkle with the
water and combine until the dough holds together.
Gather the dough into a ball, wrap in plastic wrap,
form into a disk and chill for about 30 minutes in
the refrigerator.

Turn the dough out onto a lightly floured surface and roll out to fit a quiche dish. Chill in the refrigerator while you prepare the filling.

**For the filling:** In a bowl, whisk together the half-and-half, eggs, pepper, salt, and thyme. Set aside.

In a large skillet, heat the butter and olive oil over medium heat. Add the pancetta and sauté until crisp. Remove the pancetta with a slotted spoon and set aside. Add the leeks to the hot skillet and sauté until tender. Remove the leeks with a slotted spoon and set aside. Add the artichoke bottoms and sauté until lightly golden brown. Remove the artichoke bottoms with a slotted spoon and set aside.

Remove the crust from the refrigerator and sprinkle the Monterey Jack cheese evenly into the bottom of the crust. Evenly layer the pancetta, leeks, and artichokes over the cheese. Pour the egg mixture into the crust. Sprinkle the Asiago cheese on top. Bake for about 35 minutes, or until the custard is set and the top is golden. Let cool before slicing into wedges.

*Serves 6*
*Serve with Valley of the Moon Winery*
*Chardonnay*

1996

CHARDONNAY

NAPA COUNTY 45% • SONOMA COUNTY 27% • SANTA BARBARA COUNTY 28%

ALCOHOL 14.1% BY VOLUME

## VIANSA WINERY

*On the evening of January 29, 1988, on a hill near Sonoma, Sam and Vicki Sebastiani opened a bottle of sparkling wine and toasted the land that would one day see their dream a reality. Their winery, Viansa, would embody a proud Italian heritage, and it would overlook a lowland shared by vineyards and nearly 100 acres of restored natural wetlands. Today, Viansa is a reality welcoming visitors from around the world, and they invite you to share your wedding, special event, or meeting with them. The wines and food of Viansa are among the world's finest, and the wetlands provide critical habitat to countless waterfowl, animals, and aquatic life.*

# POLLO FARE
# MERENDA
## *(Picnic Chicken Smokies)*

*These chicken rolls are a favorite for picnics since they taste great served at room temperature. This recipe is from Cucina Viansa by Vicki Sebastiani.*

6 large chicken thighs, boned with the skin left on

2 tablespoons Viansa Hot Sweet Mustard

1/4 cup minced white onion

3 tablespoons freshly grated Parmesan cheese

Salt and freshly ground black pepper to taste

12 small (1-inch) smoked sausages

1/4 cup Viansa Winery Chardonnay

3 slices bacon, cut in half

*(recipe continued on next page)*

Preheat oven to 350 degrees F. Lightly oil an 8 by 8-inch baking dish.

Lay out each chicken thigh, skin side down. Spread each thigh with 1 teaspoon of the mustard. Sprinkle evenly with white onion, Parmesan cheese, salt, and pepper. Place 2 of the smoked sausages in the center of each thigh. Roll up each thigh to enclose the filling and secure with toothpicks. Place in the prepared baking dish seam side down. Pour the wine into the dish. Top each chicken thigh with a piece of bacon. Bake for 25 minutes. Remove the bacon and bake an additional 20 minutes, basting occasionally. Let the chicken thighs rest for 15 minutes before removing the toothpicks and slicing.

*Serves 6*
*Serve with Viansa Winery*
*Chardonnay*

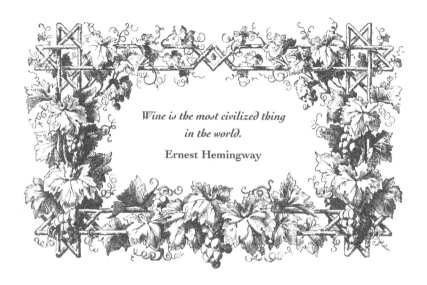

*Wine is the most civilized thing*
*in the world.*

Ernest Hemingway

# THE WINERIES:

Atlas Peak Vineyards
3700 Soda Canyon Road
Napa, CA 94581
707.252.7971

Beaulieu Vineyard
1960 St. Helena Highway
Rutherford, CA 94573
707.963.2411

Belvedere Vineyards and Winery
435 West Dry Creek Road
Healdsburg, CA 95448
707.433.8236

Benziger Family Winery
1883 London Ranch Road
Glen Ellen, CA 95442
707.935.3000

Buena Vista Carneros
18000 Old Winery Road
Sonoma, CA 95476
800.926.1266

Canyon Road Winery
19550 Geyserville Avenue
Geyserville, CA 95441
707.857.3417

Cardinale
Post Office Box 328
Oakville, CA 94562
707.944.2807

Chateau Montelena Winery
1429 Tubbs Lane
Calistoga, CA 94515
707.942.5105

Domaine Carneros
1240 Duhig Road
Napa, CA 94559
707.257.3020

Dry Creek Vineyard
3770 Lambert Bridge Road
Healdsburg, CA 95448
707.433.1000

Ferrari-Carano Winery
8761 Dry Creek Road
Healdsburg, CA 95448
707.433.6700

Fetzer Vineyards
13601 Eastside Road
Hopland, CA 95449
707.744.7600

Frey Vineyards
14000 Tomki Road
Redwood Valley, CA 95470
707.485.5177

Geyser Peak Winery
22281 Chianti Road
Geyserville, CA 95441
707.857.9463

Glen Ellen Winery
14301 Arnold Drive
Glen Ellen, CA 95442
707.939.6277

Gloria Ferrer Champagne Caves
23555 Highway 121
Sonoma, CA 95476
707.996.7256

Handley Cellars
3151 Highway 128
Philo, CA 95466
707.895.3876

Kendall-Jackson Wine Center
5007 Fulton Road
Santa Rosa, CA 95439
707.571.8100

Kenwood Vineyards and Winery
9592 Sonoma Highway
Kenwood, CA 95452
707.833.5891

Ledson Vineyards and Winery
7335 Sonoma Highway
Kenwood, CA 95452
707.833.2330

Louis M. Martini Winery
254 South St. Helena Highway
St. Helena, CA 94574
707.963.2736